True News

Craig Watson

Instance Press
Santa Cruz, CA
2002

Some of these works have appeared in:

Windhover, Shearsman, untitled, First Intensity, New American Writing, Cross Cultural Poetics, ENOUGH

Cover Design: Courtney Watson
Art: Barbieo Barros Gizzi

Instance Press
327 Cleveland Ave.
Santa Cruz, CA
95060

Instance Press titles are available from:
Small Press Distribution
1341 Seventh Street
Berkeley, CA 94710
(800) 869-7553
orders@spdbooks.org

CONTENTS

SPECTACLE STUDIES

WHERE/AS

HOME GUARD

for Chris, Courtney and Sofia
"first this world..."

I don't want to come, yet suddenly I'm here;
I don't want to leave, yet suddenly I'm gone.
Don't know where I've come from or gone from, either.
In this there is, of course, True News.

—Yuan Mei
Trans: J.P. Seaton

SPECTACLE STUDIES

polis is spoils

—Ted Pearson

PICTURES OF THE HANGING

The world precedes us, if only
In steps, but we acquire a body
By elimination, momentum by
Displacement, union in quarantine.

Every wall protects
But how small is reason perfect?
Stories accrete into pictures
That infinity of the under-imagined.

So does margin imply center or
Can knowledge parent release from
Reflection's aggression, each moment
Convulsed to undestruct, sheer to extant?

Between white noise and carrier frequency
We inhabit a language of sheer proposition.
History has been consumed but
Our ears are still carnivorous.

PROBABLE CAUSE

Theory peeked out from behind the curtain
And whispered "welcome—you don't belong here"
Then resumed "the production of meaning."
Is there ever a moment without regret?

Like those pears reduced to pictures
Or birds with large eggs inside them
We forage and discard
One hollow bone at a time.

Pleasure is what we're looking for:
A horse in the dark or that which
Thought erased; horseness, darkness.
The sign of endless pause.

But who will hear us coming out
Their eyes, every opportunity despoiled by
A crash-and-burn grammar, as if one could
Make *white* equal the word for white.

ARTIFICIAL RESPIRATION

A shot rang out: let's communicate.
No form, no thought, that's clear.
Every story betrays its teller.
As if we could possess the way we die.

An adjective visualizes its prey.
Names clot perception.
This may be how we know we're alive
In the comfort of a blank canvas.

Now you can write that biography
The one without the pronouns or
A mirror in which you can't see yourself
Only what's behind you.

Memory is the birthright of longing:
A crime of passion and luxury,
That certainty disproportionate
to its own shadow.

PLACEBO

Push needle through eye.
Are you still "a man"?
Conscious and dead
Or unconscious, alive.

An electron cannot be described.
But even an inanimate object is full
Of movement the way floating
Wreckage floats apart.

One audience deserves another:
Every spectacle conceived in
That loving complicity of beliefs
And unanimous acquittal.

Now let's focus, let's addict.
Placebo means "I will please."
Hail to these, our faithful copies:
Kill one and let the other go.

PROFIT MARGIN

Every choice is a round trip
From wilderness to climax
Among a knowledge that exerts no gravity
Between seeing and the thing seen.

Like a perfect virus
Or a bride in the dark, we want
What anyone wants as if
The reciprocal was always true.

Only the author can escape
That chorus of particulars and
Rain from below, a continuous
Failure which keeps us immortal.

Nevertheless, we dig and fill
Burn and pour, haunted by
The act of acting and the inequity
Of eternal solace.

PLUS ONE PLUS

To locate a unified single subject
Fold and tear moon from earth
Or imagine us endowed with aboriginal fertility
Scratching with pointed sticks in the dirt.

We like to think that fantasy battles reality
Because pictures easily adapt themselves
To any available space and every
Silence imitates a freeze-frame consensus.

But the dead hate that metaphor of sleep
As if each absence implies enclosure
Or a class of images craving projection
Back-lit by the verso of chance.

Eventually we will return to the senseless
That home-away-from-home prose
And prescient fear of falling between
Unequal half-hours and every flawless deceit.

COMM.

Dear echo: shut up.
What you call writing we call waiting.
Now tell us the story of the future familiar
Or who do you want to fuck.

At last we can see what a goal solves:
A bird instead of flight, a house
Of temporary separate angles
One gene pool in perpetuity.

Put that in your own words.
Every question ends in a question
And description offers a rent-to-own option
Of spontaneous doctrine and simultaneous translation.

Later, we will turn into an occupation
And organize a government self-legal
From simple grammar and private perjuries
That is, survival by the neck.

OBEDIENCE

Dear F. Fatale: why do animals wear masks?
The first men lived in complete harmony
With god and nature while they
United with monkeys and bears.

Now, in the lost language depository
Dismemberment is the first goal of science
So the eyewitnesses can only identify themselves
While chaos looks the other way.

Even breath is male or female,
Thrust or rejection and each mother-tongue
Grinds salt from ruthless ambition
Object to subject and back again.

But no sex today, thanks anyway.
This narrative has emptied our bodies
And only the missing link remains
As if we are still devolving.

PATH OF LEAST RESISTANCE

Thought engraved a devoted world
For each blind and celebrated image.
So we consigned our trust to ambition and
Applied for citizenship in the wax museum.

Just as a picture becomes unanchored from
The idea of a picture, the more we learn
The greater becomes our ignorance, until
Each resemblance creates another, unconditionally.

In a perfect world, witnesses are
Nothing more than indestructible puppets:
They receive thought, crack heads, then walk
Into the past precisely where the past is.

Eventually, we will substitute the figure
Of many with the word for empty.
Anonymity will be our just reward:
That blessed purple match head.

MISSING AND PRESUMED

Everyone in this picture is gone;
That's what it takes to invoke the world.
Truth could be the law of the father
Or a rock in a rock storm.

A map's red lines display shortest distances.
The blue ones tell us what to think.
Why "parent" rhymes with "parrot" and
How long the dead remain dead.

There are always three choices:
The feast, the ordeal, the cul-de-sac.
Meanwhile, every lyric impulse
Caresses the dirt in our mouths.

If this is where light comes from
Then music must be an echo of the big bang
And a new prime number can only exist as
Infinity regained, a place to hide in broad daylight.

WITH CERTAINTY

In the manifesto of happiness
The sum of all words inhabits a solid distance
Where each effortless destiny is indivisible
By the muscle that slowly chokes it.

From orthodoxy stammers privilege.
This is why hands do not have faces
And fractals crumple against every riveted eye.
A map without destination, a gift unoccupied.

Subsistence sung a cool profit.
Now name this ambivalence:
The detective in search of the detective.
The potential of the glass unjuiced.

In the end, architecture will triumph over
That duality of mind and resurrected spirit
By which we imagine ourselves outside form
And shadow: all lips, tongue and teeth.

ANTHEM

Years pass and symptoms fade.
We exchange hand for thorn
Grapes-for-kisses and love letters
To strangers scratched in acid.

To invade a body made of body
One must embrace fruit as fruit,
Dreams as parasites, and every disease
A cornucopia of self-sufficient commerce.

But who could have known
That temptation would fill the ballast
And each moment of "here" would reconceive
The future, claustrophobic with purpose.

Now imagine the tyranny of constellations
And the culture of each receding silhouette
Where the absent share their crumbs
With those who starve them.

HOMESIGN

Thrown soap broke the silence.
A trilobite crossed the road.
Consider these the literal facts which
The horizon could not keep out.

But what was the source of light
Behind those pinholes? We knew better
Than to call them home despite that sticky
Public dark between likenesses.

Each hope cultivates hope
A sense altogether senseless.
So we converge the way a camera summons
To imitate the life that would exclude us.

Neither chance nor choice,
Desire will always eliminate itself.
In the republic of replica
What repeats becomes real.

2/15 OF A SECOND

A newborn "O's" her mouth
To the hums of passersby.
The natives are restless:
All praise hopeful monsters.

Express yourself.
Subscribe yourself.
Today, like yesterday
An insolvency unendured.

In the desire machine,
Hunger forms flesh.
One window conceals another
Gathering a familiar light.

According to reason
God has no mouth but
In the river of stain
Everyone's name is each other.

PROOF

Glorious sunset, brilliant clouds.
The air is growing but these days are
Only half-filled, the edge of one splitting
As it rises and slides over the other.

Observation demands congress.
But a way of being is not a way of seeing
Unless we inherit the glue and enact
A limit equal to all our misgivings.

Can a fact change value, auto-
Erotic to possessive, infinitely divisible
And spilt from one gap into another,
Drops-to-dreams-to-dark rivers.

From a violent dawn
To a day that is wrong,
Substitute strategy for a world
Surrendered to belong.

RESTITUTION X

A butterfly beats its wings in China.
This is/is not an emotion.
"Nothing out there, no one in here."
Property doesn't lie.

In the next room one boy stabbed another.
Someone had scrawled "kiss" on the wall.
Back at the station they'll study the pictures.
But if we look at a river do we become a river?

Natural time socializes historical time.
Each gesture cuts the distance in half.
God created law but is above it and need not obey.
Only failure revenges expression.

A civilian steps off the sidewalk.
This is how a day legitimizes a life.
Seduce your assassin.
Motive will replace us again.

WHERE / AS

Four Geographies

VENICE
for Patti

Look what a mess we've made: lost Dante in the boat, drank from canals, learned original sin by example; then, while asking for directions, we were handed history without a bilge pump and hung from our heels across the bridge of sighs.

A road is the archetypal metaphor for change, but this city is all shadow and steam so we move easily between islands, leaving no wake in water and no echo against fog.

In some languages the same word means *sink* and *swim*,
but who were they talking to, so attractive and absent?

Even if we never see it coming, happiness knows what to expect; but we dwell in the gap until we can calculate an escape.

As the voyage progresses, the scenic absorbs more of itself: mountains of sunflowers block the sky, a detour celebrates the denied destination, landmarks erase the map.

It takes an image to make an image,
each fact sculpted from another's surrender.

Someone must have imagined a world made of inanimate parts: first a wilderness untitled, then membership, competition and reward; that is, everything that we're fighting for in mock perfection and blind orgasm.

This must be the triumph of retreat, failed by a doubt, resilient as a tongue under house arrest.

Morning's oil fills the moat,
each monument having to be slid across.

On purpose then we would not be wandering to document the
unthinkable, knowing how predictably a narrator-in-fact resumes the
concatenation-of-crimes in thousandths-of-seconds.

So how to read the story of civilization gone-to-ground as that
myth which makes sense of holy war, or a collective prayer in which the
accursed name the bereaved.

Perhaps it is a particular type of air that becomes dark, sleep
deprived, as absolute as one more point of reference in an imagination that,
once we get there, is no longer possible.

In the factory of glass, every story is a self-portrait in which the tellers compete with the listeners for a single moment impregnable to catharsis.

A new order will replace the old: ice makes more ice, property provides traction, memory conserves memory; soon we will all be joined at the teeth, ravenous and indivisible.

But for now we will accept narrative for spectacle,
blood for razor, obedience for a pool of used light.

Trance for trance, the opposite gleams in perfection, as if something that had never been done could be effortlessly recreated.

In the house of conjugation, each word is written over another: the ink of ages dries on pages undifferentiated between points-of-reference and random profanity.

Some languages require that every name have a gender, but once it was possible to imagine a middle sex so one of every three propositions was true and silence was just another tide.

These days, however, the public demands 360-degree communication: mouths take seed from strangers and appetite swallows itself in piecework-to-practice starvation, that monotony disguised as will.

Together we unthought the act of love,
but a leap seemed too lovely to refuse.

Does makes right
for every new emblem of totality.

But no one wants to be a subject, that sanctioned exuterine tableau: a-passenger-on-a-train watching a-passenger-on-another-train, someone exchanged for someone else, someone after.

Blunt instruments carve the afterlife so we must make reliquaries to protect this world from the next: a clock without hands, a desiccated womb, a book of erasures to remind us of those barbarous days.

Slowly the streets become sentences, crowded with greetings, regrets, best wishes, until our words can't be used against us and the least of all opportunity becomes the most absolute.

On a wall discarded by an empire we scratched our initials so we will have an alibi when the foundation finally sinks and the treasury is sold for clean fill.

This is the compromise between suicide and amnesia,
that is, what we meant without saying so.

Even though a secret can't hurt us, breath soaks phosphor from message dust, all traffic and product blind, until, given the givens and minus the contingencies, the fix is in.

Eventually we will put on our clothes again, as if to replace bond with bondage and reclaim what we could not conceive, for instance, that unrelenting thirst at the bottom of the sea.

Ghosts tell stories to become unnarrated, mouth-to-mouth in a film running backwards, every antecedent unoccupied, free from their lungs turning blue.

We intended to reveal our pleasure in that hole where no "I" appears; then our blackmail was returned as *undeliverable* because we misspelled "margin" for "imagine."

So if there was nothing here before, and then nothing after all again, what happens next will always happen, a city in the hollow of a hand.

Later architects will build a new world
in which history is devoid of change.

SOUTH AFRICA
for Paul Maseko

Falling through the veneer of one sky
we sprawl on the surface of another;
in the garden where we were born
we return to where we've never been.

Torn tree horizon, cradle of bones, huge yellow teeth star the dark;
there are two Africas: the first reconstructs an ancient image of natural
order, the second consolidates it in the last person through the door.

Thus came the great revolutions: the trees tumbled into the grass
that had strangled them and our progress was marked by a ceaseless quest to
dig in the ground and chop meat from bone.

But who can refute with certainty
that a leopard can become a bird
or a person will change
the shape of the sky?

Even before we arrived
and painted our teeth red,
a thick white tablecloth smothered the castle,
False Bay to Impossible Island.

In a properly domesticated memory, matter is interchangeable, so in order to narrate a desire called "terra incognita," history invented the present, that generous father whose continuous gaze impregnates his children.

Now we can draw a new map, one without center or margin, and mark the four cardinal directions: "do not enter" "do not exit" "do not belong" "do not come back."

To enact an imitation nature
we have created a perfect language
in which absence is the key
to every material lock.

Any nation could be a metaphor
for a journey between parentheses,
but this was always a landscape
crowded with missing forbears.

Yesterday it was too hot to search for survivors, but we found a
message on the back of a torn photograph: "there's no point writing this
because there [sic] going to kill us anyway."

So is it possible to conceive a silence that excludes all others; after
all, now we're part of the solution and the problem is just an empty holster
on a pair of desert fatigues.

There is no doubt that every story
inhabits a different host:
the local is always primitive
and the future is forever inconsolable.

To be uninvited means many things
so we have no choice but to identify
with the arbitration of our conquerors
until we can break their thumbs.

After all, what would be a relationship without authority or a labor
perfectly divided from purpose: our a cappella promises, their click-and-stamp-
their-feet; our simple right to murder our parents, their lascivious venomous
beasts.

Nevertheless, just as water poured over a ghost reveals its shape, we
wear our humanhood for every occasion: mercenary, missionary, anthro-
pologist.

The only question now
is how to reassemble
our unconscious mind without
exposing the names of our patrons.

A tribe of ancestors make camp, sing songs
and reload their slingshots; if we stay
where we are and don't ask questions
they won't find any use for us.

So we awoke in the shade of the prehistoric world and tried to
rekindle a sign that could save us: "who is your father?" "what river do you
drink from?" "do you mourn for the proximate anew?"

From time to time paradise gets mislaid; every representation also
represents itself because the inevitable cannot be tested and even a cured
patient incarnates death.

We have been reborn countless times,
obdurate and voluptuous;
now who has the strength
to perform another autopsy on himself?

Some songs have no melody:
we inhaled those one-of-a-kind flowers
which give off exotic perfumes
and instant poison.

Thus repelled, we swam the last few miles between windows until we found the river where two oceans meet; even before the first greetings reached us, we had nothing in common.

We thought we were piecing together what had been falling apart; then a corpse on the veldt made us change direction and compose a new anthem to terror.

But who was that streaking
through the Olduvai dawn,
blood-in-the-eye for
spear-of-the-nation?

Zulus on the move burst thousands
then disappear to get necklaced:
some sang the hymns, others hacked the fields;
some wrote the book, others buried the guns.

An act of genocide can be refuted with a new definition of genocide; each atrocity succumbs to a photograph of ideas.

An audience moves to its boundaries then looks back towards a vanishing center; this is the great and beautiful hoax perpetrated by the speculative grammar of ordinary meaning.

So how do we narrate annihilation
as distinct from an off-course safari?
Thank God our traditions have been destroyed for us,
and we don't have to do it ourselves.

The need for stories invented power,
first to distinguish people from animals,
then to mark and separate
humans from each other.

Desire colonized imagination, plastic and tenacious, as if we needed to inhabit someone else's thought in order to become ourselves, forever and untold.

In a garden of boundless complexity, the namable exists only to reflect the unnamable; tonight we will walk through a desert made of paper, into a dawn that will refuse to admit us again.

This is where children
died for language
in order to bite the hand
that counted them.

A snake comes out of its hole
goes around a tree
and back in the hole.

To capture the cage, invite the beast.

As we are sheltered, so sustained; perhaps there is already too much
to remember.

The center of a circle in a square in a circle:
everywhere to fall.

Translate this:
freedom is sleep in reverse.

Though we arrived without being able to speak, we could effort-
lessly pour the contents of one cup into another.

The quiet plural around each cacophonous finger.

Now translate this:
the sign for many,
the sound for empty.

A silver moon shot the window.

On an island surrounded by land
there are only two alternatives:
outside and outside.

Even upside down, everyone touches the ground simultaneously,
the true imperative of a waking trance.

Though we are vigilant and ubiquitous
reality has nourished our misunderstandings.

Cloud horses return from a heroic age
with regards from fortune-the-unrepentant.
How can the past be improved on?

   At the end of every epoch, tombs were emptied and monuments
leveled; all the historians had to do was redistribute the wealth.

Only the holy have entered here,
and none have ever returned.

The public loves a hole.

The name of this opera is
"Finding the Leader of a Coup d'État."

With each new sleight of hand
desire seduces fear
leaving a skeleton every mile.

Next time, we will become exactly who/what we thought we were:
half a mouth, a twisted foot, an audience reflected in a painted eye.

Breathe sky, until gone.

Ink is water haunted by a failing light but we had already emptied
our lungs and looted the tombs at leisure.

The 10,000 years.
Waiting cuts rock.
Rock cuts flesh.

In a tangible present,
we inhabit a vacancy between symbols.

Is it earth or world that would obliterate us?

Vegetal or bestial, the army never really had a chance: swords rusted, bows rotted, horses on their knees.

The goal of simulation is saturation.

So what shall we use to represent
the cow that bore the first bull or
the treason of unrequited desire?

Victory is civil as communion is not.
"No fail, no veil."

Some gestures falsify
a world that hasn't happened yet,
metric-to-blur.

So we cut the space the only way we could, or thought so at the
time, then left to find the place that left us and then leave it all over again.

If the imagination is a subject without an object,
what possibility does the physical displace?

An accident waiting to happen.

Cloud broke, wave froze
tooth and blade
whetted on the bone of
the back of the world.

Stars between islands
corners and steps;
this is the
closed country.

Then we crossed a cold equator and fell through a vertical horizon,
that sentence behind the sentence, breathless.

Nowhere else
above.

Awake all night in
wet cement and choked barks,
arrested between sighs
for promises to harden.

Then sour milk and
cash exchange:
knives, cloaks,
anonymous witnesses.

We had heard how, when surrounded and outnumbered, conquis-
tadors invited their enemies to dinner then beheaded them with salutes.

Wait in the mist and
see what chance can do.

Is family learned
or instinctual:
to sleep on any pillow as
the sum of untold distances.

Knowing how rain can split a mountain and
how a mountain can fill a sky and
how a sky is neither pavilion nor abyss and
how an abyss enters mouth and throat, all gravity.

Between the mud factory and a path paved with last intentions we changed languages, then whispered into the deafening drone, foreigners again.

That which we inhabit
inhabits us.

To keep a secret
one story must be true and
another false or at least
as invisible as the obvious.

These children float
drop-by-drop, ghost-to-glass;
not rain but always
the color of rain.

After the king was allowed to fill a temple with his own ransom he
was offered a choice of implements, sashes and cords, for his garrote.

Here means one way
to go or the other.

Tongue slipped in toe hold
so climb among
words through
crevice and plunge.

Learn to say "please"
"thank you" and
"the way your mountains
prove the earth is flat."

These are the illiterate pictures of beauty without desire, longing
without a mask, allegory for every new name alight.

The wind is
a moving hole.

A squared arch to
a trapezoidal door to
a circular tomb where
even breath cannot slip between stones.

The shadow of a giant condor
rorschached the sun
but we went on burning
the rope bridge at both ends.

In the fortress of no resistance, gravity denied the distinctions but
we learned to swallow our echoes; admission will be free but there is no
refuge.

What if
we were not yet born.

A boy with a gun
hummed an imported tune
intended to enforce
the deadly peace.

There was no end
to the thirst or
the sweet salt
that drank it.

So we galloped hard through a desert thatched by root and vine,
gold-fields and landing zones, cemeteries and monkey markets, toward a city
at war with itself.

Always the same gesture to
take the world and give it back.

Every day the cloud factory
draws a new map
and asks "who goes
and who goes further?"

Then what to leave
behind: our furniture,
our food, our voyage
without wake.

It is simply the world that always wants more of itself so that we may
someday resume the point of no return and count our blessings where we left
them.

Those who cannot go home
already are home.

HOME GUARD

What have we managed to
change but the surface?
—Eléna Rivera

Figure B

In the next 60 seconds we will begin our descent; instinct says "confess now." It is one thing to fantasize a destination and another to go "out there." Of course, the same can be said of memories: they lie then forget their lies in that continuous foreplay which converts natural resources into ready-mades. On a high shelf, almost but not quite out-of-reach, we've stacked chipped trophies, desiccated nests and other misplaced genitalia. While the universe drifts toward greater order, chaos starts here, in the wake of what hasn't happened yet, each freedom crossing the empty threshold of our hands. Home is everywhere we are not; just ask anyone who refused to take our word for it.

Figure C

According to the Bible, every picture has a sound; a miracle boxes the airwaves daily. Applause masks the drone but our antennae are pre-tuned to the new Esperanto so we can distinguish between durable goods and siren songs without having to apologize all over again. Now any civilian can be a majority or own a language, each unfathomable certainty calling forth the invisible in all its picture-perfect glory. Nevertheless, the hard labor of a few supplies melody to the many and fresh-born babies regard the announcers as their fathers and advertisers as their mothers. For now no one regrets the Age of Prophecy but next time we'd prefer no dust in the ears, or perhaps dust, but no nouns.

Figure E

Thank you for your generous contribution but now we'd like to black that moon and turn up the bass track so these theories start to bleach before someone puts an eye out. They say the devil's in the details as if spirit has form and virtue is immutable but how will we know when we're not at war or that it's time to roll over in our graves and return to the palm of God's divine impotence? For now, we'll have to be content by stacking sandbags on the gallows and eavesdropping on the detainees. Though we don't want to be tempted, we like to watch, and the end of the world will be no different from any other deus ex machina: scissors, paper, rock.

Figure F

A family presumes ancestors, uprooted and exiled, every generation multiplied by strangers from an involuntary tide of common conduct and judged by spectators nostalgic for a survival predicated on each other's failure. Name lays claim to body: father, daughter, another child of preference, each rechristened into the clan-state of nurture-without-nature in full camouflage. Loving and insidious, the avant-garde of filial truth always trumps the slow agriculture of insatiable nostalgia. After all, the pencil that began this letter has long since disappeared between the rubber and the road so someone yet unborn will have to write *DEFAULT* in these blanks in order to break the back of habitual antecedence.

Figure G

It is one of the particularities of spectacle that every utterance, disgorged claw-to-fang or mimetic as sacred silence, forms a new center-of-gravity in the shifting trinity of witness, victim and shame. On television, particle waves inhabit space as anchors and borders so every image of separation is replaced by ideologies of assembly. The asylum of victory is obvious to anyone who repeats this homily: "the friend of my enemy is the enemy of my friend." Wealth, comfort and applause have replaced illusions of immortality and thereby freed the sheep from ownership and made them man-eaters again. In this virtual paradise, the future lives on its reputation, thematicized by the sign of nature, ex officio.

Figure I

We would like to think that the ocean is various from its contents so it would be flotsam that tells stories and thereby maps the void. Into this treasury are placed recollection, rapture and the grammar of gratuitous seduction. Between any two points hides a third conceit: contingency indentures faith to reason until the messianic absolute cannot be separated from its demonic twin. That is, everything we imagine becomes true and like those blackened bones between stars, the complete book is always elsewhere. Heaven is fungible and if we are guilty it is for what we lack, not what we've done.

Figure J

After the stoning we exhumed the adulterer as wave after wave of charity wafted over the audience. Nothing completes our humanity so much as property deconsecrated in the pursuit of empathetic novelty. Then the desert backdrop fell, revealing a new infrastructure of high morality and the best of infotainment classics. Having no use for a community that is not vicarious, we licked our knives and fled the theater; later, self-expression found us picking up pennies for luck and food in the parking lot. In the library of the impending world, carriers control content and the news cycle is always on mono to ensure we pledge allegiance to each perfect arc of representation, gone to ground.

Figure K

The duty of sex is to initiate the proletariat into the monastery of free credit where the past can do no harm and everyone learns to sing "be happy in defeat." Ours is a supernatural destination of recycled necessities, smart bombs and closed captions. In the genetics lab the logicians misread consequence for coincidence, so what had been sacred was simply pregnant and unfucked. Back on the street, among the sounds of sales cultivation and public burnings, it remains impossible to imagine one as another: that which doesn't so much resemble as replace. Here we can disappear among the clones that metastasize to the sign of themselves continuously asking: which of us is the other, desperately?

Figure L

We wondered as we wandered but when we reached the kill zone the republic had been privatized and the theme parks had adopted a damaged-goods-no-return policy that reality-checked every identity. On the wide screen, the death toll looked almost real, as if the yellow tape was all that blocked our view. Would-be survivors addressed their final testaments To Whom It May Concern as if they knew that the only hope was the idea of hope, an anarchy unrequited. Later, under the flat light of a frozen moon, perhaps after the sortie rate has decreased, we may be able to distinguish between shadow and stain, cathedral and tomb.

Figure M   *for Sarah Ruhl*

The purpose of a soul is to divide the map; each blessing cuts the distance in half then half again, until, as in any practical economy, the guest must eat his host. If struggle is the pursuit of advantage, the devil's greatest trick was not the substitution of mirror for method but welding the mask of sympathy to the body of necessity. Despite the triumph of a perfect rehearsal, the essential is always anecdotal. Like that old song about one fish in the mouth of another, we are not accountable for received distances. We will know that our journey has ended when we see slag pits glowing in the distance and jet wash scrubs the film noir from our eyes.

Figure N

By definition one can't prove intent though there is no reason to feel remorse unless, of course, all suspicions are well founded, as they usually are. A safe haven could be the future taking place or that calm before all the breath in a civilization exhales simultaneously. Like ideas ripped from headlines or medicine's poison flooding an incontinent heart, our best creations are those that replicate us. So leave that trumpet next to the milk bottle; although the tune has been recreated, we can still hear the slaves sing about the promise of reparations. To control history we must divide the crisis we cultivate from the crisis we advertise and thereby know when to worship the dead and when to eat them.

Figure P

In the small world so attractive to shareholders, war manufactures new consumers so a good enemy replaces the gold standard with the erotic amnesia of no-risk investment. This is not meant to criticize the work force which aspires to consume that which it must continually produce: a renewable past which promised limitless growth. Human nature, it turns out, is based on dependency and every obsession needs a collaborator. As with marriage, when an icy hand gropes for an invisible thigh, only limits lack self-knowledge and theft always comes easier to a man of faith and taste.

Figure S

In the beginning the world was nothing but river and it flowed in every direction at once so the will of the river was the will of the world and nothing else. Then moveable type replaced gunpowder as the universal cash crop and the sun-of-science never set on an unlicensed public domain. Even the grand stories of exploration and conquest now only appear as surplus photographs of that which has yet to be subdued: oceans to plains, hostiles to intimates, property that belongs to property. But not all service sectors are created equal and the mystery is not so much knowing what's going to happen next as sentimentalizing it. Although fear rules the nation, it does not rule itself: they are the government, we are its people.

Figure X

A hand passes from the practiced form of each usage to the potential signature it engenders; this is called the cycle of growth and remission, appropriation and loss, consolation and paradise. In an unpopulated conscience there is no distinction between an act and an object, so it is impossible to measure the proper relationship between the living and the dead except by their semblance. Neither an image of divinity nor stories from the animal farm will help us reconcile that mill of imperfections between two tongues. With the confidence of a born criminal and the claustrophobia of a loyal virgin, we continue to dissemble imagination with its pseudonym.

Figure Y

The old fruit-and-vegetable economy dried up and blew away but self-defense gave us a way to sell average desecration at high-end prices. Even a short stroll through the new merchandise will expose the rationale for our revolution. To the marooned, an island is nothing less than the literal center of the world, that regenerating museum which scrawls an ideal past from a relentless and irreducible present. Nevertheless, the cause is always greater than the means and those who prophesize self-determination are doomed to endure it. Today it's Christmastime on Earth so we are safe from friendly fire and we can begin to revenge ourselves on our diagnosis.

Figure Z

The answer is no and always will be. A new chance leaves others behind so after every counter-counter-revolution we comb the fields for evidence, the thing which belonged to somebody else. Though we would like to rely on the good will of others, a sovereign middle is the class of all other classes, one that does not subscribe to any example. Are we here yet? Or still in the grasp of the analogous universal, that impassable predicate of open space and common ground where tomorrow is forged from collective memory. Our sole aspiration is to sustain an innocence, gnostic and harmonic, until we can return to our lesser instincts intact.

Also from Instance Press:

The Habitable World by Beth Anderson

Haunt by Keith Waldrop